ODYSSEY OF WORDS

IQRA ANSARI

Dedicated to my mother

& everyone I've lost and gained this year

Contents

Contents

Foreword

I write these words
for the ones
with art on their arms,
a stroke for each broken moment.
I want you to know,
you are the most beautiful painting in the room.

• x •

• x •

IQRA ANSARI

Iqra Ansari is a self-published author of Oxymoron. She has been writing for over 8 years, as a hobby, and finally took the leap to self-publish. She has written fiction for years in additional to original contemporary romance and romantic suspense stories.

She is currently working on a stand-alone full length contemporary romance and have started outlining the fantasy romance story.

She loves telling stories and creating something that allows people to go on a journey of the mind. She has co-authored anthology like "The Warrior Heart", "Shajar Lafzon Ka", "The Hidden Hero". She is about to publish her second fictional novel, The Eve, a different kind of love story.

I WISH I COULD TELL YOU

1. I WISH I COULD TELL YOU

I wish I could tell you,
How beautiful you are
I wish I could tell you,
I love you more than anything I could.
I wish I could tell you,
Your laps comfort me more than any expensive mattress.
I wish I could tell you,
Your food tasted super delicious then any fancy restaurant.
I wish I could tell you,
I search you in every crowd.
I wish I could tell you,
Your smile feels like blessings from heaven.
I wish I could find one perfect word that can describe you.
I wish I could tell you my upcoming journey,
But now, all I can do is wish if I could tell you.

SINCE I'VE MET YOU

2. SINCE I'VE MET YOU

Your abode is with me,
Looking for your lane, I found my house
You hold the meaning to my life.
Looking for you I finally found my lord.
Since I've met you, I have become capable
Since I've met you, I've achieved it all
Since I've met you, I've become more of myself.
Since I've met you, I started living whole.
You made me realize my worth
Gave a reason to my earth
I know I am nothing,
tomorrow someone might arrive as a replacement,
but in my heart your place will remain constant.
For a world I am just human,
For you, I am a poetry.
and that's what I always wanted to be

IS IT THE MIRROR, OR IS IT JUST YOU?

3. IS IT THE MIRROR, OR IS IT JUST YOU?

Is it the mirror, or is it just you?

You make me look better every day.
Why do I think about you all the time?
You're like the ocean;
And I am like the thrashing waves
You're a world of emotions;
While I am just a little speck.
Is it the mirror, or is it just you?
You make me look better every day.
If you're lost,
I am willing to take care of you.
Slowly, dwell in my eyes.
And come live in my dreams.
And come live in my dreams.
I would be there in no time, even if you call me in your sleeps.
I am sand and you are an ocean
I am sitting on your shores.
Is it the mirror, or is it just you?

You make me look better every day.
If you're alone in the journey
I am the solution to that loneliness
You would feel me, if you can read my feelings.
I would spend the night lying on your chest
And I would tell the mornings not to rise in my city
Is it the mirror, or is it just you?
You make me look better every day.

"

"

IQRA ANSARI

ANGEL

4. ANGEL

Stars fallen from the universe
and Night became history
He came from heaven just to be with me
Consumed all my darks away
Without promising forever to stay
Just like broken leaf from the branches of tree
He became my strength and set me free
I wonder if he's an angel
As I don't expect kindness from humanity
All my obstacles I've been through
He stood beside me
Maybe he's an angel came from heaven just to be with me.
The darkest of my days
I had been through
I had you,
Right from efforts to my goals
Became your dream to make it true
I wonder if you're an angel
God sends at night to make peace within
Or you're just a lot a ocean
Finding it's wave
Maybe you're the edge

I found when I was drowning in life's cyclone
Or you're someone I achieved after losing all!
I may not be yours
But you're all mine

13

BROKEN PEOPLE

5. BROKEN PEOPLE

I was the sunken ship floating all over the river
You were the passenger seeking for an edge
Your efforts of not giving up
Bought all my broken parts together
Maybe that's why they say
Broken people heal each other!

DELUSION

6. DELUSION

Living in a delusion
Lost somewhere within
Even life was upset
And when the heart started loving self
Life flattened instantly
Eyes were barricaded by fog
Happiness was standing behind
Along with a smile
Even my heart said;
Listen, enemy of your own eye,
Neither I am broken nor I am lost,
Anywhere for a moment
Alone with a sleepless night
I found my morning

MAN

7. MAN

Man
Hustle for your career,
Girls isn't going to pay up for your barrier
Though you're a man
You got to wipe your own tears
You've so much responsibility to deal with
Yet you manage to put smile and care
I feel for you.

TRIBUTE TO EVERY SURVIVOR CALLED WOMEN

8. TRIBUTE TO EVERY SURVIVOR CALLED WOMEN

Oh yes..., I have been raped

I am expected to remain clean and shaved

I have been tortured for being alive

I get greeted on my pregnancy

Nobody knows how much I got fucked to gift another life

Yet I start another day with a good smile

My dupatta isn't sign of my simplicity

Nor my skirt holds a symbol of bed time availability

My incomes are said to be untouchable

Why do they look at me like I am a public property?

Why my financial status defines my independency?

They found me interesting tt

Until they're done fucking

I am not just a vagina

I am the goddess that has the power to recreate

My sex defines my uniqueness

Stop mistaking it as my weakness

I am somebody to be earned by efforts and not by expensive gifts

You want to make me feel special?

Just treat me equal, stable and compatible

EMPTINESS

9. EMPTINESS

I feel bad; I feel sad as if everything was never enough.
No matter how hard I try, it's not enough.
I feel bad; I feel guilty and sad.
I feel so empty and lonely,
I'm hungry for the company.
Not so commonly, I feel wasted.
This isn't the only bad feeling I have tasted.
My bad moods are coming to me faster,
I'm drowning in loneliness,
I'm craving for the company.
Comparing myself to others, I can't stop.
I think this was the last drop.
Tears drop my face; I usually don't let them.
My fears are coming to life,
Those wasted years of procrastination,
No one cares. No one cared.
I'm suffering; I don't know what's wrong.
Nothing seems wrong; still, I feel wrong.
I feel lonely; I feel sad; why do these feelings keep coming back?
Can't get rid of things, I can't fix.
Added into my feelings mix.
I write and write, feeling worse about myself every day.

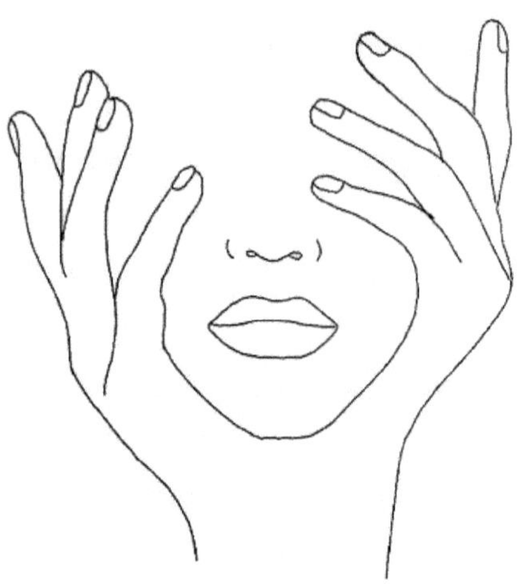

BROKEN STRINGS

10. BROKEN STRINGS

Silence

I can't take it- the silence piercing my screaming skin

Ladies and gentlemen, I don't know where to begin

For all I feel now is pain

Silence-I can't take it it's driving me insane

There is no instrument to distract the bitter thoughts

Silence-what my soul never sought

Do I have to wait to the end of time?

To stop silence's crime

To hear the slightest sound of a guitar string

I'm mad? HA I'm telling you it's not my fault!

I'm trying to hide behind a string's note

Ladies and gentlemen

Broken strings are what I've never ought

There is no sound to distract fears

Now it's clear

I have to wait for the broken strings to mend

This is something I can't comprehend

I lost my only friend

Silence- just like a dead battle field

No voices to encourage, to cheer

To erase fear

Now all I have left is the voice of my sobbing
and then I'll shed tears
For I know I can't play the broken strings

DEFINITION

11. DEFINITION

I bite my tongue
and taste my blood.
I scar my skin
and watch the flood.
I love the pain
engulfed in my vein.
An identity I was given
without my permission.
I don't want recognition,
I want a new
definition
of me.

LOST TO BE NEVER FOUND

12. LOST TO BE NEVER FOUND

I don't want this night to find its end.
I hope it is lost in its own labyrinth.
So, the hands ticking have to freeze
Leaving me alone with your company.
I'll get an extra second, minute, hour
Or an entire eternity with you
And that will be my every 11:11.
Dear moon, let me get lost in search
Of the beauty in your spots.
I want to be the one who is
Lost to be never found.
So...
I don't want this night to find its end.
I hope it is lost in its own labyrinth.
So the hands ticking have to freeze
Leaving me alone with your company.
I'll get lost in the light falling on my skin.
Or I will pour out every word
Encaptured within.
Dear moon, let me spend

Yet another sleepless night with you.
I want to be the one who is
Lost to be never found.

HE IS THE DEVIL

13. HE IS THE DEVIL

There's a voice who cries out of utter pain.
Their screeching noise is heard from all corners of the room.
They are in pain, for their wings have been sliced off,
and blood seeps beautifully from their crimson backs.
They are to be banished out of the place of beauty
and adoration for the highest.
Nobody heard them when they screamed in unimaginable pain.
No one came to their aid when they had their reputation taken
away.
No one defended them when they were cast down to live with
mortals.
No one helped them get their revenge.
As slithering and revengeful as they are, they were willing to wait
for months, years, decades, centuries.
Waiting to get back to the place they once were.
They are regarded as the fallen.
Their sins were unforgivable, their deeds were satanic.
Like the first fallen angel himself.
He is now the ruler of where fleshes burn, and humans who have
sinned scream in agony for eternity.
He revels in chaos, in anarchy, in doom.
He does not care about the inflicting pain

and the everlasting fire lashes out to the poor sinners.
His heart is as black
and dead as the people whose skin sparked with the flames,
its tongue licking their flesh, as they beg and plead in agony.
He decides not to hear their cries, because they mean nothing to
him.
He smiles when he sees them in pain.
They did what he had requested, but in the end, they got what
they deserved.
This is what they get when they worship him.
He is a traitor, right from the time he was a deceitful slithering
beast who whispered words of abhorrence to the first woman
whose feet touched the earth.
He is the archfiend
The first of the fallen
The virulent beast who lures other to commit sin.
He is the devil

• 39 •

IN MY MIND

14. IN MY MIND

I have crossed the hardest milestone I walked this path alone,
Alone with the emptiness exaggerating within,
Setting the confinement of limits.
I kept running from the wolf,
Chasing the thirst of finding a better place
I kept fighting the demons yet I couldn't win
Eyes barricaded with fogs
With no roads in between
I am haunted from the dark
& Trying to pick myself up little by little
I've spent my whole life fighting the monster under my bed
Only to figure out it was in my mind.

EVEN AFTER

15. EVEN AFTER

Even after meeting, I didn't meet-
you, don't know why, of miles-
there are distances from u, don't know why,
unknown series (of say, links) are there,
attached to you, don't know why, dreams are there-
below the eyelids, because of you, don't know why.
that who's living (can say stuck) in my eyes,
that looks exactly like you,
I don't know whether your eyes or talks were the reason,
that you became the wish of heart,
you, even though near,
you, even though wished for,
even after being a feeling,
are not mine, why do I have such complaints,
against you, don't know why, of miles,
there are distances from u, don't know why,
you don't know.

DEATH WISH

16. DEATH WISH

This curse of a body
And this torture of a mind
Leading me closer to a coffin
I'm starting to think that it's a sign
maybe if I close my eyes
his voice won't echo anymore
maybe if I end my racing mind
I will have stopped it from the core
maybe god hates me because
I've been mean to myself
but this mind belongs to a sinner
and that's the only way it would be dealt
the body he touched
will fade from this world
my eyes will turn liquid
So, I won't see him anymore
I won't dream, I won't hurt, I won't suffer
I won't have to listen to my own sadness's clatter
I will be free
of his promise to fix me
I remember, i held both of his hands
And he saw it in my eyes, he was my only chance

he was my god, my miracle, my hope that the world finally
understands
but how could I believe I'd be set free
when I'm the prison?
and so he left like the change of a season
and now I'm cold
a corpse
a living dead among the living
a beating heart that barely works
I hope your god is more forgiving

NOW LAYS TO REST

17. NOW LAYS TO REST

Though we've had our fair share of hard times;
I truly wish you the best.
I think you're amazingly incredible,
Though our friendship now lays to rest.
I'm happy that we've resolved things,
Learned a lot and grown,
Our maturity and selflessness
Has finally been shown.
So, to my old friend,
I hope for you amazing things.
We all have incredible in us,
Now it's time to let it sing.

KETKI

Hello, my name is Ketki and I am a writer. I have always been fascinated by stories and the way they are able to transcend time and culture. My hope is to be able to share my love of writing with others and help them see the world in a new light. In my spare time, I enjoy reading, traveling, and spending time with friends and family.

HER

18. HER

If it's hard to fall in love
then maybe I never learned how to patiently wait.
I remember your hands
wrapped around my waist
and I felt them around my neck.
since that day there has been an
intoxication in your smile
that once shined brighter than death when I let her free.
Now that I have fallen for you
I think of you from sun rise to sun set
Day and night like a prayer
My heart whispered
Make her your habit
Hold on to her
I'm addicted to you like
I am with the music
I silently sob to
you are a drug
but it feels like I
can never get enough
I want you,
the taste of your lips,

the smell of your perfume
and your breath against my neck
oh, I feel you in my veins
and every vessel is in ecstasy
I'm losing control
and I'm feeling every effect
The flames we marched through,
the oceans we crossed,
the rain that poured Down on our fragile hearts,
the storms we faced.
It was worth it.
Because at the end of the journey I found the other half of my
soul.
And we created a new path,
together, hand in hand.
It's indescribable
I just can't describe it
How amazingly awesome
My love is for you
I just can't find the words
To say my love for you
Is bigger than the world
Would be an understatement
Even to say I love you
Can't express how much
I care for you
And how much I appreciate you

Sometimes I even think
That my love for you
Isn't enough
But you manage to convince me otherwise.
As always.

APURVA PITALE

Apurva have done her Masters in Sociology. She has worked in media for more than five years and now she works as a lecturer. Writing comes to her naturally. She expresses herself through writing.

DISENGAGEMENT

19. DISENGAGEMENT

I have changed they say,

the naive,

unquestioning girl they wanted me to stay.

Everyone has an opinion my on how I live,

But now that I am cold, I have no fucks to give.

Emotionally drained,

I am a detached freak,

Gone are the days when I was labelled as weak.

Some say I put up a rough exterior,

I do cry, it's just that I shed no tear.

Darkness is now my comfort zone,

Light, well that I have outgrown.

I shared, I shared but nobody cared,

In this ruthless world, my heart I bared.

Now they question my disengagement,

But they are the ones who cause a dent.

VAL SHELBY

Val is an aspiring writer from Mumbai. Lives on coffee, music, machines, and escapism. Lives for today's sunshine and tomorrow's mystery.

Some write because they must, some write to put their thoughts into the world, and He write for the love of it.

SHERIDAN PINE ANNIE

20. SHERIDAN PINE ANNIE

East Coast Valley,
West of Route Eighty-Nine,
There's a sleepy little town
Called Sheridan Pine.
My heart skips a beat
As I pass the old sign.
There lives the girl of my dreams
Whom I am out to find.
Seven winters spent together
Playing in the snow,
But the last of those games
Was a decade ago.
Oh, this isn't a dream.
I might be out of mind.
But I am looking for Annie from Sheridan Pine.
Her hair would reach her shoulders,
Deep red like her mother;
She was as tall as I was;
Eyes deep blue like no other;
Last name was "Martins",

Had a dog that was blind,
I am looking for Annie from Sheridan Pine
Been visiting my favorite aunt
That first December
I was only fifteen
Nothing else I remember
Save for the young girl next door,
She was so cheerful and shy,
I learnt that was Annie from Sheridan Pine.
Friendship seemed to blossom
Seven Christmases came round
Oh, we were holding hands
As we walked about the town
Warm feelings abound
Snowy butterflies, a sign
I am looking for Annie from Sheridan Pine.
We'd hike up the hill
On deer trails at first light
The town would vanish in the mist
Then glow in the sunshine.
Campfire by the river
Hash-brownies and cheap wine
I am looking for Annie from Sheridan Pine.
It's a town from an old song
Of broken hearts and wings
I could play it on guitar
But only Annie could sing.

We'd write a few songs ourselves,
About two hearts entwined.
I am looking for Annie from Sheridan Pine.
Falling off bicycles
Ending in matching plaster casts
Turned into cars in a ditch
Because we were laughing too hard
Going too fast, even on uneven inclines
I'm looking for Annie from Sheridan Pine.
Jumped into the river,
We were cold for a week,
She said she thought it'd be funny
Meanwhile I couldn't speak.
She might be crazy too, but she's one of a kind.
I'm looking for Annie from Sheridan Pine.
Old sweater, new boots,
Red ribbon in her hair,
The last time I saw her,
Voice filled with despair
She said she'd be gone too,
Leaving this town behind.
I'm looking for Annie from Sheridan Pine.
She'd talked about it before,
When we'd stare at the sky;
She saw her name in the stars,
I'd simply wanted to fly.
The first time we kissed

Was a bittersweet goodbye.
I'm looking for Annie from Sheridan Pine.
Here I am now,
The place is eerily still
An old man says, "The quaint old town
Has moved over the hill."
Seeing the records store all boarded-up,
My memories rewind.
I'm looking for Annie from Sheridan Pine
Leave my truck along
The ancient army airfield,
I set out on foot.
The night starts to yield.
The mist rises up,
To catch the moonshine.
I'm looking for Annie from Sheridan Pine.
There's a new road ahead
Rub my hands and fight a shiver
Walk down an old trail instead
Spot a campfire by the river
She's alone, has changed so much
But I recognize those eyes
There she is, my Annie from Sheridan Pine.

• 67 •

ABHIRAJ DAS

Hello, my name is Abhiraj and I write. Writing has always been a passion of mine and it's something that I love to do. It's a way for me to express myself and share my thoughts and ideas with the world. I started writing as a teenager and since then, I've continued to write every day. Writing is my life and it's what I love to do most.

SOMEWHERE

21. SOMEWHERE

Let's go to a place where the impossible becomes true.
a place of mixed dreams and reality for me and you.
We can be '70s detectives trying to solve a case,
or we can be disease-surviving teenagers trying to escape a giant
maze.
We can fall into a rabbit hole and eat cakes that make us shrink,
we can discover a kingdom in an old wardrobe that makes us
not want to blink.
We can be wizards or muggles being sent to school to learn spells,
or we can be pirates heading to 'neverland' on a ship with
canons and barrels.
We can be demigods, fighting with our swords and winged-shoes,
or we can be shadow hunters hunting and looking for clues.
We can search the paper towns of New York to find the love of
your life,
or participate in 'the selection' for the prince's quests for a wife.
We can be dead souls looking down as our sister depicts the
mystery of our death,
or be a dauntless, an erudite, a candor, or a mix of all that.
We can be peculiar kids trying to fight of the 'hollows',
together with the other peculiar children and everyone that
follows.

We finish our quest, flipping through the last pages,
closing the books we will remember and love for ages.

• 73 •

NO CAGE CAN CONFINE YOU

22. NO CAGE CAN CONFINE YOU

You can't be fat,
You can't be flat,
You can't be short,
You can't be too tall.
Don't wear short skirts,
Don't wear tight jeans,
Show your skin? No way
Consult the books of Sanskaars.
Don't wear too much makeup,
Don't wear too little,
What makes you is your outer shell,
Without it, you'll be just an object to dwell.
How late you reach home,
How often you booze,
Don't you know?
These are scales to measure your character.
This entire world is full of lies,
It hides behind a cruel guise.
Your fate doesn't lie in another's hands,
Society isn't the judge, before you stand,

Never think that being dictated by it is okay,
It deceives you to believe that it's the only way.
O Angel, no cage can confine you,
O Angel, no person can restrict you,
O Angel, no chain can bind you,
Realize that this is true.
Spread your wings wide,
Break all the barriers and fly,
With your dreams, give a ride,
To the soaring sky.

• 77 •

GLASS SKIN

23. GLASS SKIN

These walls are too high
Too close, pressing too hard.
I am suffocating on my own
Words, let me out. Please.
I need to find a road that leads home.
But this is my home, I'm stuck
In between two worlds
I love and hate Life and death.
In a state where I am both
Alive and dead, free and trapped.
My body can move freely
But my mind has gone to hell.
My thoughts spill out
Of my mouth and eyes.
I am poisonous, I bite.
I am both a rose and a grenade.
I don't want to hurt you,
I am Possessed.
I am afraid you will trip
Over my shattered skin and bones
And break yourself.
I love you too much

To inflict even a drop
Of pain upon your small body.
My tears are made of venom,
I am more beast than human.
Leave this house.
Leave me.
Leave us.
Dig a hole in the backyard
The size of my body,
I'll take care of the rest.
There is glass near the door
Don't step on it
On your way out.

MARVELOUS LADY

24. MARVELOUS LADY

Pretty ladies wonder where my mystery lies.
I'm not adorable or worked to suit a design model's size
Be that as it may, when I begin to let them know,
They believe I'm telling falsehoods.
I say,
It's in the compass of my arms
The traverse of my hips,
The walk of my progression,
The twist of my lips.
I'm a lady
Marvelously.
Marvelous lady,
That is me.
I stroll into a room
Similarly, as cool however you see fit,
Furthermore, to a man,
The colleagues stand or
Tumble down on their knees.
At that point they swarm around me,
A hive of bumble bees.
I say,
It's the fire in my eyes,

Furthermore, the blaze of my teeth,
The swing in my midsection,
Furthermore, the delight in my feet
I'm a lady
Marvelously.
Marvelous lady,
That is me.
Men themselves have pondered
What they find in me.
They attempt to such an extent
In any case, they can't touch
My inward puzzle.
When I attempt to demonstrate them
They say despite everything they can't see.
I say,
It's in the curve of my back,
The sun of my grin,
The ride of my waist,
The beauty of my style.
I'm a lady
Exceptionally.
Exceptional lady,
That is me.
Presently you get it
Exactly why my head not bowed.
I don't yell or hop about
Or, then again need to talk really.

When you see me passing
It should do right by you.
I say,
It's in the snap of my foot heel,
The twist of my hair,
the palm of my hand,
The need of my care,
'Cause I'm a lady
Amazingly.
Amazing lady,
That is me.

FEEL EVERYTHING

25. FEEL EVERYTHING

Does this feeling ever go away?
the one that comes after fear
the one you never thought you'd feel
it isn't even a real feeling, is it?
because in order for it to be real
you'd have to feel something, right?
and right now, I feel numb;
I feel nothing.
for the longest time
I wanted to feel something
other than despair
and I feared that
it would never go away
but perhaps
the greater fear is not feeling anything
at all
because who are we without emotions?
there'd be no anger or hate or sadness to feel
but there'd also be no love or happiness or joy
and if I've learned anything

while in this dark tunnel
of isolation it's that
I'd rather feel everything
than feel nothing at all.

THE LAST FRIEND

26. THE LAST FRIEND

I feel stupid, and I feel sad,
You're not the last friend I've had,
And I'm not mad.
I'm just sad.
And it's my fault; everyone left me.
This friend theft is my fault.
I should have been a better friend.
Why did I always criticize you?
I wish I could apologize, but it's too late.
Will you say now, "Bye-bye, mate?"
You made a new friend.
Am I replaced now?
I don't feel relaxed.
My sadness has been released...
Is it your or my fault?
Do I have the right mindset?
Should I blame myself?
I'm feeling fine.
I mind my own business.
I'm ignoring what's going around.
Tears don't make a sound.
You made me a wound.

Is it my fault?
Now I regret what I did.
Can I start anew and forget?
Will you forgive me?
Or was it me who didn't forgive you yet?
Or did we not forgive each other?
Why is it such a bother?
I shouldn't care, I shouldn't see.
But I still ask myself... "How dare you?"
I shouldn't care. I shouldn't see.
I shouldn't let it affect me.

LET ME SLEEP

27. LET ME SLEEP

A clear whisper,
Dancing in my head,
Go to sleep love;
Your eyes are dripping red,
A shallow cry,
Resonating my heart,
Don't put me to sleep;
I may never wake up,
A mirthless laugh,
Escaping my soul,
Why bother to sleep;
Let insomnia keep you warm,
A silent scream,
Clawing my chest,
As I lay here awake;
Wishing to be dead,
Don't let them come,
My eyes protest,
I beg my nightmares;
Please let me rest,
Why is it so hard?
Closing my eyes,

Escaping into a land;
Where my sky won't cry,
Numb with struggle,
To just fall asleep,
Even for a second;
Let me sleep not dream,
Burning with fear,
Fighting all alone,
Fearing the shadows;
Hiding in my home,
After all those nights,
Just this time,
Please let me taste;
What peace feels like,
My vision blurs,
Tears slide down,
I can see them coming;
They want me to drown,
Can you hear me?
I'm calling for help,
Don't let them take me;
They'll drag me to hell.

REMEMBER ME

28. REMEMBER ME

Remember me,
when my words
no longer rhyme.
When I lose
all I ever had,
remember me.
When my poetries
become fragments
of my memories,
remember me.
When I cease to exist
and my words are the
only pieces left from me,
remember to remember me.

GHOST

29. GHOST

You know what a ghost is?
Someone who almost
found his home
but utmost
never did.
He hangs around hidden,
afraid to loosen the grip.
You know what a ghost is?
Someone who almost
drank the water
but utmost
never did.
He hangs around hidden,
afraid of losing what
he thought he owned
when he never did

THANK YOU

30. THANK YOU

Thank you for staying with me,
Thank you for sticking with my attitude,
I don't have any other words to say than thank you.
Because I believe it, I'm really thankful to you.
I'm too thankful that you came into my life.
You became my light when I was locked in the dark,
You became my happiness when sadness was eating me,
You became my hero when a villain was trying to hurt me.
You're always there when I needed someone to hear my story,
You're always there when I needed someone to hug me after I cry,
You're always there when I needed someone to say that it's going
be okay.
I'm thankful that, once in my life, there's someone,
Who made me feel I'm special.

YOUNG HEARTS

31. YOUNG HEARTS

The words that mean everything in the world but seem so much but so little at the same time.
The easiest of emotions to feel but the hardest words to say.
The words that only should be said when you truly mean it.
I wonder if there is such a thing so perfect but yet you're tormented.
There may be ups and downs, fears and tears.
Passion and hate romance and jokes. But aside from all that, the main thing is how you feel.
The world may tumble down on you both but if your bond is not strong I guess you weren't meant to be.
Your hearts may be broken but Someday you will find your match, the one you hold forever, cherish and adore.
I remember the day you said those words but she couldn't say them back.
She broke your heart and crushed your spirit.
All is forgiven.
Remember after all we are young hearts set on a goal.

ABYSS OF MIND

32. ABYSS OF MIND

*And I'm finally set free from the abyss
of my mind,
There where my darkest thoughts
roamed free,
Where those contradictory voices
we're screaming and laughing at me,
There where the shadows of my demons
consumed me—almost completely—
But when I finally fought back...
They feared ME,
And I became their queen.*

Dear Reader,

Let me ask you something — who is the writer without their readers? It is an eternal question — would art exist without spectator? I don't know the answer. But I know that every time I write — I write with my readers in mind.

Readers are the writer's mirror — in you, we see the reflection of our words and ideas. You help us to shape them, translate thoughts into sentences and communicate them with you.

Knowing that there are people who are genuinely interested in the ideas that we share makes it a whole more interesting. It creates a space for conversation - writing is not a monologue.

It's an indescribable feeling to know that you've touched someone's life, maybe changed it a bit or just gave them a reminder of a thing that they've already known.

Writing makes us friends with the people that we've never met and probably never will. In connects and unites us no matter where we are and who we are.

So thank you, dear reader!

* 9 7 9 8 8 8 7 3 3 0 8 6 0 *